A Suitcase of Seaweed
&MORE

ADDITIONAL SELECTED TITLES
BY JANET WONG

Poetry Collections
Behind the Wheel: Poems about Driving
Good Luck Gold
Knock on Wood: Poems about Superstitions
The Rainbow Hand: Poems about Mothers and Children
TWIST: Yoga Poems

Picture Books
Alex and the Wednesday Chess Club
Apple Pie 4th of July
The Dumpster Diver
Homegrown House
This Next New Year

Chapter Books
Me and Rolly Maloo
Minn and Jake
Minn and Jake's Almost Terrible Summer

Books on Writing
Before It Wriggles Away
You Have to Write

The Poetry Friday Power Book Series (with Sylvia Vardell)
HERE WE GO: A Poetry Friday Power Book
PET CRAZY: A Poetry Friday Power Book
YOU JUST WAIT: A Poetry Friday Power Book

Other Poetry Anthologies (with Sylvia Vardell)
GREAT Morning! Poems for School Leaders to Read Aloud
The Poetry Friday Anthology (K-5)
The Poetry Friday Anthology for Celebrations
The Poetry Friday Anthology for Middle School
The Poetry Friday Anthology for Science
The Poetry of Science

A Suitcase of Seaweed
& MORE

Janet Wong

Y U Z U
An imprint of Pomelo Books

TO ANDREW

AND WITH GRATITUDE
TO RENÉE M. LATULIPPE AND SYLVIA VARDELL
FOR THEIR "2 CENTS"

Author's Note: Now and then you may wonder why I put a poem in
one part of this book rather than another. Sometimes the reason is
as small as one word, or my memory of a certain salty smell.

YUZU
An imprint of Pomelo Books
4580 Province Line Road
Princeton, NJ 08540
www.PomeloBooks.com
info@PomeloBooks.com

Library of Congress Cataloging-in-Publication Data is available.
ISBN 978-1-937057-33-6

Please visit:
www.JanetWong.com
www.PomeloBooks.com

CONTENTS

About this Book

A Suitcase of Seaweed was originally published in 1996 by Margaret K. McElderry Books, an imprint of Simon and Schuster, as thirty-six poems plus three prose pieces.

The entire text of the original book is presented here with new text added in gray boxes: you'll find snippets of story about the inspiration behind the poems, extensions of the themes, and general musings. I've also included prompts to get you thinking and talking—or even writing. I would love it if this book inspires you to write your own book, too.

In the almost-final draft of the original version of this book, poems were presented all together, not divided into sections. When I asked my editor Margaret McElderry if I could illustrate the book, she answered, "This book does not require illustrations, but if you really want them, you may do them—three very small drawings, black-and-white."

How was I going to choose which three poems to illustrate? That's when I decided to divide the book into three parts, with a prose piece and a drawing introducing each section. I have always been very aware of the three different sides of me—Korean, Chinese, and American—so picking three section themes was easy. Sorting the poems was much harder. Sometimes all three parts of me called out to claim a single memory, like three teams competing in the Olympics. Did the right team win each time? You be the ref.

If you were asked to divide your identity into three parts,
what would you say?
Mom-Dad-You? Child-Friend-Student? Serious-Silly-Silent?
How would you like to be seen?

7

Part 1:
KOREAN POEMS

Garlic Boat   JW

MY MOTHER IS KOREAN. She came to this country in 1960, having recently married my father, who met her when he was stationed in Korea with the U.S. Army. I still am not sure how they met, exactly. Something about him buying food for the troops and her selling food from her farm. How could they fall in love, since she could not speak English and he could not speak Korean? He married her for her nose, he says. It is a pretty nose, short and thin, pointed, straight. I have my father's nose.

Growing up, I never felt very Korean. My Korean aunt and grandparents lived in this country for only a few years, when I was in high school. And I visited Korea only once, when I was four. The month I was there I learned to speak enough Korean to order ice cream at the train station. It was the best ice cream I have eaten in my whole life.

Lately I have been wanting to know more about my mother, and for the first time I find myself craving Korean beef bone soup and kimchi, which I used to hate. Now I can eat the hottest kimchi without wincing. I eat it whenever I like, not caring about garlic breath, even turning down the gum the waitress offers when you pay the bill. Gum won't work, anyway, once garlic gets in your blood.

My mother once warned me not to eat kimchi before an important meeting. "You don't want garlic breath!" Last month I spoke at an evening program where there were many Koreans in the audience. I made sure to eat kimchi during dinner—one whiff and they'd know I was authentic.

But I'm not always so bold. Recently I was on a plane, seated near the front of the coach cabin. I stood up to go to the bathroom in the back, but then saw that the aisle was blocked with a cart. I hesitated, trying to decide whether to go later or to try to use the first-class bathroom, and then decided to head to first class. At that same moment, a man walked up behind me and grunted. I looked at him; he motioned dismissively for me to step aside. I let him pass, reflexively, without thinking, giving him access to the bathroom first. I was raised to avoid conflict. *Don't make waves.* A woman seated nearby made a comment. It was a comment of solidarity meant to support me, but it made me feel weak. I regretted letting him go ahead of me (and not just because he took a long time).

Too often, those of us who are polite and introspective worry about bothering other people. We skip the garlic because someone might not like the smell; we step aside and let rude people get their way. Maybe we need to start asserting ourselves more. Carefully, because there will be some people, especially rude ones, who won't like it and might use their power to harm us. But let's be clear: it's not just about me eating kimchi or her wearing a hijab or them being together as a family; it's about all of us being able to be our true selves in peace, whatever is in our blood.

What part of yourself do you need to assert or protect?
What's in your blood?

LOVE AT FIRST SIGHT

I like to imagine Mother
when her face was full and smooth
and she wore her hair in a long braid,

and I like to imagine Father
with his crooked smile and his crooked crew cut,
wearing an American uniform,

running after her
in the narrow dirt streets
of her Korean village,

as she rushes away
laughing,
her long braid

wagging like the tail of a dog
that has found
a fresh bone.

When my father was in the U.S. Army in Korea, he somehow convinced his commanding officer to give him a pass every weekend so he could leave the base to buy fresh food for the troops. I'm sure my father used that pass to do lots more than just shopping—but I guess the sergeant didn't care as long as my father brought back loads of fresh eggs, meat, vegetables, and fruit.

I can imagine him clucking like a chicken laying an egg, mooing like a cow, pantomiming a fish being caught, hamming it up and making all the farmers laugh. The first day she met my father, I'll bet my mother laughed a whole year's worth.

With all that laughter and joy in the air, how could they not fall in love?

Think of your parents or any loving couple that you know.
What do you think brought them together?
What things make them a good couple?

BURIAL

We take turns
digging the hole
in the hard dry ground,
pushing the shovel down
in the dirt
with the soles
of our shoes.
The sweat drips
from my forehead
into my eyes
like tears.
Slowly Haraboji
lowers
the large clay
kimchi jar
into the cool dark pit,
this makeshift cellar
where chili peppers
and garlic and cabbage
will mix and sit in salt,
covered
with snow until
spring, when
the kimchi is hot enough
to chase away all
trace of winter's
chill.

My mother was born and raised in rural Korea, in Geumsan and Gimje. I went with her to Korea when I was four years old to visit my grandparents. The city of Seoul, half a day away on a slow train, was in the process of becoming one of the sleekest cities in the world. Parts of Gimje were starting to become more modern, too—but not my grandparents' farm. Their house had no electricity or running water. Their toilet was in a shed where the chickens and pigs lived. Water for washing, cooking, and making barley tea was pumped daily from the well. There was no refrigerator. Food was dried on straw mats on the ground or roof, or preserved in jars underground. There was a charcoal-fired oven outdoors, near the porch, that also heated the floor of the house.

We ate kimchi at every meal along with little dishes of fresh vegetables—kongnamul (mung bean sprouts), spinach, squash, peppers, and eggplant. Our protein came from steamed eggs or dried seafood. My favorite dessert was sikhye, a sweet rice drink.

In 1994, the Simon and Schuster copyeditor for the original version of this book made me italicize the word kimchi because it is a foreign word. *Kimchi.* You never see pasta italicized. Or croissant. Or sauerkraut, which kimchi is (with the addition of red chili pepper and garlic). In fact, kimchi has become common in many American cities, where people eat it because of probiotics and gut health. Do you think we might even see kimchi in the school cafeteria one day? I hope so!

What are your comfort foods?
If you were required to eat one healthy thing at every meal—
always the same thing—what would it be?

LEECHES

With his cigarette
Uncle Kishunee
burns them off
my legs
one by one,
smearing
their marks
with mud.

Then he carries me
home, piggyback,
along river rows
of grassy rice,
his bare feet
sucking
the ground
like leeches.

One day during my visit to Korea, my mother told me that we were going to walk through the rice paddies, and I had better keep on moving so that "worms" wouldn't attach themselves to my legs. The only kind of worm that I had ever seen in my whole life was a regular earthworm, which couldn't attach itself to your body. I didn't know what my mother was talking about. She didn't know the English word for "leeches." I didn't learn that word until I was twelve years old and read it in a book.

I was just four years old at the time and I kept getting tired and distracted. The mud was so heavy. My feet would sink into it and I would have to lift them out; each step felt like ten steps.

While my mother and my uncle marched ahead, I stopped often, stooping to splash around. An hour later, we found leeches up and down my legs. Thank goodness I didn't sit in the water.

Have you ever had a leech or tick stuck to you, or lice, or another kind of parasite? Have you ever seen a person act like a leech?

ACUPUNCTURE

"Chook! Chook! Chook!"
Mother says each time
she digs her finger
into my skin
to show me where
the doctor stuck
hundreds of needles
in her swollen, still,
fever-filled body,
when she was twelve.

I have a picture
in my mind
of how she looked—*Chook!*
My mother, once
a porcupine.

I sprained my ankle very badly when I was a teen. My mother decided that acupuncture would be the best treatment and took me to a Korean acupuncturist on Western Avenue in Los Angeles. I had never had acupuncture before. I was a little afraid, even though she had told me the story of how acupuncture healed her when she was a child.

The needles hurt, maybe because I was so tense. (I've had acupuncture many times since then, and usually the needles don't hurt at all.) Between the acupuncture and RICE (Rest, Ice, Compression with a bandage, and Elevation), I got better in a few days.

It's possible that my ankle would've healed just the same without all that, too. Some people say acupuncture only works if you believe it will.

When you have been sick or injured, how have others helped you heal?
When others have been sick or injured,
how have you helped them?

A Suitcase of Seaweed

Across the ocean
from Korea
my grandmother,
my Halmoni,
has come—
her suitcase
sealed shut
with tape,
packed full
of sheets
of shiny black
seaweed
and stacks
of dried squid.
We break it open,
this old treasure
chest of hers,
holding
our noses
tight
as we release
its ripe
sea smell.

We were waiting for my Korean grandmother at LAX, the Los Angeles airport. It was Halmoni's first trip to the United States. We spotted her coming out of Customs, dragging her heavy suitcase. It was almost bursting, held shut with duct tape; lucky thing the Customs officers didn't require her to open it. I guessed that it was filled with presents for me: traditional Korean dresses called hanbok, which are quite large and puffy; traditional Korean shoes, shaped like canoes; maybe Korean paper fans, too, which don't fold up. When we got home, we cut the suitcase open with a knife. *Seaweed?! Squid?!!* I was so disappointed.

It was 1975 or 1976. Halmoni had brought these things with her because she remembered receiving letters from my mother, years earlier, about how she couldn't find any of her favorite Korean foods in America. Now there are dozens of Korean grocery stores in Los Angeles, but in 1960, when my mother first arrived in this country, there were none.

For many weeks I refused to eat the seaweed, squid, and fish. I was angry that these things had taken up space in that suitcase—a suitcase which should've held dresses for me instead! In the end, though, I ended up loving the dried squid. My mother cooked it by holding it over the open flame on our gas stove. The tentacles curled up crispy and charred. She tore the squid up into thin strips. *Yum!* It was better than the best beef jerky.

Your family is moving to another country for a year.
You don't know a whole lot about this place, but
you know you won't find your favorite foods there.
What will you pack in your suitcase? Chocolate? Cheese?
Will people look at your suitcase and think you are strange?

CAMPFIRE

Just think—
when Mother was my age,
she could build a fire
with sparks from rocks,
catch a bunch of
grasshoppers and
roast them whole
for a summer
night's snack!

"Get me a good stick,"
she says, "thin but strong,"
and I bring her one
from the woods
behind our tent.
On the way back
I see a brown bag
by her feet—
could it be?

When the fire is spitting ready,
she reaches
in the bag, rustling,
and hands me
one big, fat, luscious
marshmallow.

The first time we went camping, my mother told me the story of how she roasted grasshoppers when she was a child. I thought it was disgusting until she explained why she did it. She grew up on a farm, so they should've had plenty of food —but this was the time of the Japanese wartime occupation of Korea, and much of their food went to the soldiers. Some nights, all they had to eat for dinner was a small bowl of rice. My mother, from when she was five years old, learned to catch food and cook it for herself. She would catch a fish, build a small fire on the riverbank, roast the fish, and eat the whole thing. Or, if she couldn't catch a fish that day, she would catch grasshoppers.

When we went camping, my mother loved building our fire. It was always a great fire. And we always roasted marshmallows—never grasshoppers, which was perfectly fine with me.

Think of a resourceful person you know,
someone who didn't always have it easy.
What are some things that person did to survive?
What are some things you've done to deal with a difficult situation?

Beef Bone Soup

It is three-thirty in the afternoon
at the Korean soup shop. Mother
has ordered her favorite soup,

boiled until the cloudy broth turns
the creamy color of old teeth. I pull
a beard of noodles from the bowl

before I remember we must pray,
and there it stays, dripping,
hanging near my chin, while

Mother bows her head. She bends
over the bowl so long and so low
she seems to be steaming

her pores open. My wrist is stiff.
I drop my noodles, hoping she will
get the hint, then I start to play

with the salt and my spoon.
But she remains as she was,
at least one whole minute more,

until I cannot help myself,
and sneak one small early slurp—
so hot it burns my tongue.

Bone broth is really good for your health but, like many things that are good for you, it takes a lot of time to make. My mother used to make her own beef bone soup, but not very often since it took three days of boiling, cooling, skimming the fat, and then repeating and repeating all of that again. It would steam up the windows and the cabinet doors; later in the week, you could see where little streams of cooled broth steam had trickled down.

When a restaurant specializing in beef bone broth popped up near us in Los Angeles, my mother was thrilled. Beef bone soup restaurants often serve only that one item on the menu: bland bone broth with noodles and thinly-sliced beef in it, salt and scallions in little bowls on the side.

My mother prayed before eating any meal, but for some reason she would pray an especially long time when we had beef bone soup. She really did look like she was giving herself a facial. (By the way, bone broth contains collagen, great for your skin.)

Is there a certain food that seems almost "sacred" to you?
What foods keep you healthy?

JOYCE'S BEAUTY SALON

They call my mother
the perm lady, "Pum Ajima."
Dozens of mad Korean women
come in each month, ugly,
furious with their families,
frustrated by their stubborn,
straight, heavy hair.
A few hours with Mother
and they leave
carrying a lighter load,
their carefree curls
bouncing out the door.

My mother was a hairdresser. When I was a child, she owned three different beauty shops—one on 8th & Vermont in Los Angeles, another on 3rd & Alexandria, and one in San Rafael. When I was in high school, she no longer owned a shop but gave perms in our garage to Korean women from her church. Forty years ago, there weren't very many Korean women in our town (Walnut, a suburb of Los Angeles that is now very Asian), but they all had the same short, curly hairstyle, courtesy of my mom.

Our family room was right inside the garage door. I would sit there doing homework or watching TV, listening in case my mother called me for help. I could hear the women in the "salon" shouting and sighing *Aigoo!* ("Oh my God!"). They definitely had a lot of frustration that they were happy to release in there. It was like having a Korean TV drama playing live in the garage.

What makes you feel happier when you are angry or frustrated?
Is there something you can do—or someone you can count on—
to help you "carry your load"?

KOREATOWN

Koreatown
is growing

like an amoeba, engulfing
whole streets each week—

        churches
        swap meets
        barbecues

        cleaners
        markets
        beauty shops

Koreatown is growing, spreading,

splitting.

I lived in Los Angeles off and on from the early 1960s until the mid 1990s, and even though I now live in New Jersey, I visit Los Angeles at least once a year. I've seen Southern California's Koreatown spread from a few stores on Olympic Avenue to hundreds of stores in a five-mile radius—and beyond. You can find stores with Korean signs all over Southern California.

When there were only a few stores, the Korean community was very tight. We couldn't go into a supermarket without running into someone my mother knew. This was not always a good thing; almost every time we ran into someone she knew, they would speak in Korean to her. I would stand there, like an obedient daughter, and say nothing.

Usually they knew that I couldn't speak Korean, but partway through the conversation they would look at me and ask (in Korean), "Doesn't she speak Korean?" My mother would look so ashamed. She would mumble (in Korean) that I was studying French and German, but—no, I did not speak Korean.

Once I told her to tell them I was mute. She looked at me, exasperated, and did not say a thing.

Is there anything about you that embarrasses someone close to you? Is it just their problem, or also yours? Do you want to try to change things—or not?

Hospitality

My guest
must not have noticed
how I removed my shoes
as we stepped inside my house.

My guest
must have missed
the neat line of freshly shined shoes
near the door.

My guest
apparently did not see
my mother's shock as she watched
his shoes walking toward her,

muck-covered shoes
impossible to ignore
when she offered him
nothing to eat.

I grew up in a "shoes-off" house. We could walk around the house barefoot, in socks, or in slippers. All our outdoor shoes were arranged in shoe cubbies or on the floor near the door. Our floor was always clean.

My husband, who is of French and German (Alsatian) heritage and grew up in a fourth-generation American household in Michigan, Illinois, and California, has never lived in a "shoes-off" house. He likes keeping his shoes on inside. When we first dated, I would take my shoes off in his apartment, but then I'd end up with dirty feet an hour later. So I gave up. We live in a "shoes-on" house, where the floor is always dirty; but actually it seems right to keep our shoes on because our house is very contemporary and the floor is bare concrete.

Probably the best compromise would be to have sturdy "indoor shoes" like Mr. Rogers's sneakers. Have you seen an old TV clip of his show? He would enter his house and immediately change from a jacket into his sweater and from hard-soled shoes into sneakers. I think it was his way of saying, "Let's get comfortable here. It's time to play." I've tried a few times to keep a pair of sturdy indoor-only shoes, but for some reason I always end up taking them outside and getting them dirty. Writing this now is a good reminder for me that it's time to try again.

What traditions do you follow in your home?
Do they make sense to you? Will you change anything when you are
in charge of a home of your own?

PERSIMMONS

Mother tells me, once again,
how *her* mother used to spy
on her, piercing the sliding
rice paper screen with a pin
and peeping through the hole
with her better eye.

That is how Mother, always
so hungry, got caught
stuffing her jacket pockets
full of dried persimmons,
and that is why I get to eat
more than anyone could ever
possibly want.

I was a fat baby. My mother would put a spoonful of food in my mouth and I would spit it out in the air. I was probably trying to say, "No more! Please stop stuffing me!"

I was a fat kid, too. My mother used to give me enormous lunches to take to school. I knew I couldn't eat half of it—I was so full all the time. Instead of wasting it, I gave part of it away almost every day. That way, I had at least a chance of eating the enormous dinners that we had at home. I think she fed me so much because she had grown up poor and starving and didn't want me to feel the pain of hunger.

As much as I really do love my favorite foods, I could never eat like my mother. She could finish ten plates at a buffet restaurant and still go back for more. If I ate fewer than three plates of food, she would frown and say, "They make money off of you!" The ironic thing is that she was always thin. She weighed less than ninety pounds for most of her life.

Think of something unpleasant or unfortunate
that happened in your early childhood.
Now imagine yourself, years later, being a parent.
What could you do to make sure that your child
doesn't have a negative experience with this same thing?

RICE COOKER

Reaching into the rice bin
with a porcelain bowl
chipped at the rim,
I scoop out
plenty for four
and pour it
in the pot.

Then I wash it,
swishing and rinsing,
careful not to spill
a single grain
down the drain,
swishing and rinsing
until the milky water
runs nearly clear.

I measure the water
with my knuckle,
plug the cooker in,
press the button
and wait, wait, wait—

wait for Mom
to come home.

Both my parents worked long hours, so I had many chores to do after school to help keep the house running. One of my daily tasks was to cook rice for dinner. It wasn't difficult, but I didn't like doing it. Usually I would soak the rice when I got home, then take a nap or goof off for a couple of hours—and rush around at the last minute, straightening the house or starting dinner right before they got home.

My parents taught me to put "two knuckles" worth of water into the rice cooker. That puzzled me. My fingers were shorter than my father's and longer than my mother's. How could my "two knuckles" equal theirs? Maybe this is why our rice never quite turned out right.

New rice cookers make good rice no matter what you do (almost). They even make happy music. The fancy Zojirushi that I bought for my mother two years ago plays "Twinkle, Twinkle, Little Star" when the rice is done. "Come here," it sings. "Have a fluffy little piece of star!"

Who does the cooking at your house?
What are some of your favorite foods?
Can you cook them?

Part 2:
Chinese Poems

Gold Mountain Tea   Jw

My FATHER IS CHINESE. He came to this country when he was twelve. My grandfather came here in the early 1920s. He worked on a farm near Sacramento, California, for eight years, then returned to China for a visit. On that visit he married my grandmother, built a house, and had a baby—my father.

Soon after my father was born, my grandfather, my GongGong, came back to the United States to make money. He worked as a cook in a restaurant in Los Angeles. Just when he had bought a restaurant of his own, he was drafted into the U.S. Army.

After World War II my grandfather brought my grandmother and father to this country. In the 1950s they bought a small restaurant and called it "Wong's Café." I worked there one or two hours a day when I was four, five, and six years old. I would arrive before dark, after I finished sweeping hair from the floor in my mother's beauty shop three doors down. I was not a very good worker and mainly just wiped tables, hiding the tip money in my apron pockets.

I liked to talk to the customers. Albert Bell—my Uncle Al—was one of our best customers. One afternoon, before I was born, he found my mother lost on the street. He knew her from the restaurant. She spoke a little English then, but not enough to find the right bus. Al helped her back to the restaurant, where my grandfather scolded her. Uncle Al always left a big tip.

The Chinese Exclusion Act of 1882 made Chinese immigration illegal except for merchants and scholars. It was repealed in 1943; but for six decades, "Paper Sons" bought false identity papers from "Paper Fathers," laboring as indentured servants in the U.S. for five to ten years, earning no money until the papers were paid off.

When a Chinese person arrived in the San Francisco area, he would be detained at Angel Island for months, waiting for a hearing where a Customs officer would ask hundreds of questions, such as "How many steps are there from your house to the village well?" or "How many windows are there in your house?" The answers were found in a book of "facts" to memorize, given to you by your Paper Father along with your false identity papers. Your Paper Father would be interrogated separately; if your answers didn't match, you would be sent back to China or detained until someone came up with enough money for a bribe.

My grandfather received his Paper Father's book right before he boarded the boat from China to America. He asked a fellow passenger to read it aloud, over and over, very slowly, and skipped meals to pay for these lessons. This is how my grandfather learned to read.

I also learned to read and write out of necessity. My mother needed help in her tiny beauty shop. I was only four, but I would sit at the front desk with the appointment book open. Customers would spell their names; half the time, I got the appointments wrong. But my mother was a very fast worker, so double-bookings were fine.

What were your first jobs—
either for pay or just to help the family?

ALBERT J. BELL

Forty years of friendship
with my grandfather,
and still Uncle Al cannot eat
with chopsticks.

Forty years of friendship
with Uncle Al,
and still my grandfather forgets
to offer him a fork.

Uncle Al was short, with a belly hard as a melon, white hair combed back, and a bristly white mustache. He was a suit salesman at a men's store, and he always dressed sharp. His wife and his daughter came with him to Wong's Café until, within a year of each other, they both died of cancer. Uncle Al then came to the restaurant alone. On Thanksgiving and Christmas, he came to my grandparents' house.

After my grandparents sold the restaurant and retired, Uncle Al still visited them every Tuesday for lunch—and, of course, Thanksgiving and Christmas, too.

Does your family have close friends, unrelated to you,
who feel like family?

POETRY

"What you study in school?" my grandfather asks.

"Poetry," I say, climbing high to pick a large ripe lemon off the top limb.

"Po-tree," he says. "It got fruit?"

My grandfather grew up in a small village in China. His family was very poor and could afford only one year of school for him, when he was seven years old. We were picking lemons in his backyard when I first told him that, having quit my job as a lawyer, I was now writing poetry.

He was puzzled about what the word "poetry" meant. I said, "Very short stories. Very, very short." He looked puzzled, still; I think he was wondering why I would give up a good-paying job just to write very short stories. I can still see the paint-splattered wooden ladder; I can still smell the lemons.

What is your favorite subject in school?
What do you think your family thinks of that?
What is important to your family?

WHEN I GROW UP

I want to be an artist, Grandpa—
write and paint, dance and sing.

Be accountant.
Be lawyer.
Make good living,
buy good food.
Back in China,
in the old days,
everybody
so, so poor.
Eat one chicken,
work all year.

Grandpa, things are different
here.

I once asked my grandfather, "When you were a kid, what did you dream of becoming after you had grown up?" He stared blankly at me. I repeated the question in a couple of different ways. "Dream?" he said. "No can dream nothing! Just get work, make money, buy food."

By age ten, my grandfather had worked as a fruit seller, shoemaker's apprentice, and noodle maker. He left China as a young teen to work on farms and restaurants in California.

The first time he ever did something "artistic" was when he was 85 years old. I had bought him some large canvases, paintbrushes, and acrylic paints, and borrowed a stack of art books from the library. He shocked everyone; one week later, he had painted something inspired by Klee. A week after that, he painted a meadow that looked like something Monet would've done. He didn't just paint, he made "sculptures," too. One night, he ordered lobster at a restaurant and dissected it very neatly, picking the meat clean off the shell. Then he reassembled the shell and told the waiter, "Excuse me, there's no meat in this lobster!"

What do you dream of becoming or doing someday?
(More than one thing is perfectly fine!)

MONEY ORDER

We eat salt fish and rice,
night after night after night,
to save some money
to send
to cousins
I never have seen

who used our money last year
to buy a color TV,
so they could watch
rich Americans
eating
steak and potatoes.

Growing up, I felt we were poor. Truth is, we were probably firmly middle class, but my parents (like many working families) struggled. My mother, in particular, worried all the time about money.

Still, she and my father sent money "home" to relatives in Korea and China on holidays and whenever someone asked for help.

When I visited China as an adult, I was surprised to see that my cousins lived in a very comfortable home with some expensive-looking electronics in it. In fact, by the standards of my childhood, they were rich—richer than we ever were!

If you were to win a thousand dollars tomorrow,
what would you do with it?
Would you spend it all on yourself or give some money away?

SHRIMP

Around and around and around it spins
on the lazy Susan,
that last piece of shrimp.
I am too ashamed of my appetite
to look at it again
so instead I force my eyes
to wander, looking at paintings
of fish and crab and
shrimp—
Instead I look at the waiters,
walking from the tanks with nets
of thrashing fish and wriggling
shrimp—
Instead I look around the table,
measuring the hills of peeled shell
piled on my mother's plate,
my father's plate,
my brother's plate—

My brother's plate!

This shrimp is mine!

Chinese families often eat "family style," where we share food that is placed in the middle of the table. When you're at home, you might feel comfortable grabbing whatever you feel like eating, your chopsticks flying in like seagulls. But when you're eating in a restaurant with your grandparents and uncles and aunts and cousins, you might feel a little more reserved, holding back on second and third and fourth helpings until the lazy Susan has had a couple of chances to spin around.

Toward the end of the meal, as everyone tries to decide whether to keep on eating or to stop, there might be just one or two pieces of food on each shared plate. When two of you reach for the lazy Susan at the very same moment, spinning in opposite directions, both going for the last bites of food—AWKWARD!

Do you like eating "family style" (sharing)
or do you prefer having your own plate (no sharing)?
Can you think of reasons for both approaches?

AFTER A DINNER OF FISH

"A surprise for you, from the sea,"
Grandmother whispers, with a wink,
once the dinner dishes are done,
once she has scrubbed the kitchen sink,
once we have made chrysanthemum tea—

now that we are alone.

"Guess," she says, "but do not tell."
She pulls a paper napkin square
from her apron pocket and
puts it in the palm of my hand.
I shut my fingers, like a shell,
around this gift, in its disguise,
knowing what I will find there—

poor girl's pearls, cooked fish eyes.

I shared this poem with my friend Monica Gunning, author of *Not a Copper Penny in Me House*, a collection of poems about growing up in Jamaica. I said, "We'd have a whole steamed fish on the table, head to tail. My grandfather would take his chopsticks and scoop the eye out of the socket, pop it in his mouth, suck out all the goopy stuff, and spit out the eyeball."

Unfazed, Monica replied, "Really, Janet? My grandfather used to scoop the eye out of the socket, pop it in his mouth, suck out all the goopy stuff—and *crunch* the eyeball." Monica won that little contest of *whose-grandfather-was-more-shocking!*

I kept the clean fish eyeballs—the "poor girl's pearls"—in my wooden jewelry box for years. One day, when I was twelve or so, I opened it, saw a dozen cracked eyeballs staring up at me, and decided to throw them all away.

Have you ever kept a collection of unusual things,
or do you have any ideas for collections that you could start?

Tea Ceremony

"This tea costs sixty dollars a pound,"
Grandfather announces, and grunts
as I begin to pour.
This is a signal
for Mother
to look at my free hand,
a glance that lasts
long enough to scold:
Two hands!

Like a puppet
I lift my left hand,
answering her silent command
to hold the lid down,
while my right hand
tips the teapot
toward Grandfather
in a slow, deep bow.

Two hands!
I feel all eyes watching
as I cradle
the old heat-cracked cup
in soft hands of respect,
holding it out to Grandfather
like an offering
to the gods.

Some people really love eating food that was on sale, a bargain, or free, no matter how junky it may be. Knowing how little it cost makes the food taste better to them.

My grandfather was the opposite. He loved letting us know if we were eating something expensive—special tea from China, or abalone, or New York-cut steak, or super-plump shiitake "Flower" mushrooms.

If I know that a piece of food was organically grown, or homegrown with love and respect for the environment, that makes me feel good. Of course, taste matters, too!

Does knowing something about your food
make it more delicious or more special to you?
Have you ever grown your own food?

GongGong* and Susie

Susie sure is good
watchdog.
Got to be.
I treat her right.
Last night
almost
kill a skunk.

Did I tell you?
Many times
I did eat
skunk
soup.
Take out them
stinky thing,
cook
with garlic, onion.
Skunk, snake, night owl,
I eat them
all.
It was Depression time.
No work, nothing
to do.
We hunt, we fish, we camp.

Hey Susie, Susie,
want to eat
some chow
mein?

*GongGong is one Cantonese word for grandfather.

My grandfather came to this country almost a hundred years ago, in the 1920s, and worked on farms in California, picking fruit and cutting asparagus. He worked at first for nothing, simply to pay back the cost of his "Paper Son" false identity papers and passage to the U.S.—but after several years he was able to earn money to keep. He didn't keep it, though. Every time he had a little bit of money saved, he would send it to his parents in China, who were extremely poor.

In 1929, the stock market crashed in this country—BOOM! Soon afterward, America was launched into the Great Depression. Rich people became poor and many regular people became homeless. My grandfather was one of those homeless people, unemployed and without savings. What could he do for food? He used to tell a story about it—the Depression story that I put into this poem, combined with his other story about Susie.

Suppose you were suddenly homeless, hungry, and alone.
How might you survive?
Would you eat a skunk if you could catch it?

Sisters

She calls me tofu
because I am so soft,
easily falling apart.

I wish I were tough
and full of fire, like ginger—
like her.

This poem is not about a sister. I don't have any sisters. It's about my mother. I called the poem "Sisters" because I didn't want her to know it was about her.

She and I were very different from each other. I have always been a person who tries to keep peaceful, even-tempered relationships with people. She was always fiery—either loving or hating people, rarely feeling neutral about them. Though we were both short, she was tough and wiry. I have been varying degrees of plump and soft my whole life.

The image of me as tofu came directly from her. One night, she started to tell me a very sad story from her childhood—a story I had not heard before. When she saw the tears welling up in my eyes, she stopped telling the story and said, "You are so soft. You are like tofu! I cannot tell you anything." This really is a perfect simile because tofu "weeps"; if you leave a chunk of tofu on a plate on your kitchen counter, you will find it in a small puddle of water an hour later.

Maybe I should have put this poem in the Korean section, but I never ate Korean soft tofu, in soon doo boo soup, when I was a child; I only ate tofu in Chinese dishes. Besides, I didn't want the world to know that this poem was really about my mother. (But now you know.)

Are you similar to other people in your family, or not?
How are you the same? How are you different?

IN THE HOSPITAL ROOM

I turn my back
on Grandmother
as the nurse
feeds her
so she does not
see me
peeking
from the corner
of my eye
at her mouth
opening wide,
too wide,
the way a baby
opens his mouth,
not knowing
its size.

This poem is not about my grandmother. I did see my grandmother in the hospital as she was dying, but my main memory of that visit was the image of tubes everywhere, so many tubes going into her nearly lifeless body.

This poem is about my husband's stepfather; I changed the facts so that my husband's family would not know it was about Pop. My mother-in-law and Pop, her second husband, are both gone now, so I feel it's all right to let the truth come out.

I saw Pop soon after he had suffered a stroke. We visited him many times in the next few years in a nursing home as he deteriorated slowly from ALS, Lou Gehrig's disease. He was trapped inside his body without use of his arms and needed to be fed like a baby. I approached his room during one of his feedings. When I saw this, I stopped and stood outside the door so he would not see me. I didn't want to give him any reason to feel embarrassed. The worst thing about ALS is that, while you are gradually losing use of your body, your mind is clear—so, along with any small joys that you might still be able to experience, you also feel intense frustration, pain, anger, and shame.

At the end of a person's life, we usually concentrate on giving love and comfort, but I think it is just as important to focus on dignity and respect.

Have you ever seen anyone in a serious health condition?
How did you act?

Grandmother's Almond Cookies

No need cookbook, measuring cup.
Stand close. Watch me. No mess up.

One hand sugar, one hand lard
(cut in pieces when still hard),

two hands flour, more or less,
one pinch baking powder. Guess.

One hand almond, finely crushed.
Mix it with both hands. No rush.

Put two eggs. Brown is better.
Keep on mixing. Should be wetter.

Sprinkle water in it. Make
cookies round and flat. Now bake

one big sheet at three-seven-five.
When they done, they come alive.

This poem takes me back, instantly, to my grandparents' kitchen in their apartment on Gramercy Place, where both PoPo and GongGong told me many times: "Stand close; watch me." They didn't use cookbooks; their recipes were in their heads. They didn't use measuring cups; their measurements were made with fingers and sharp eyes. They wanted me to watch them and learn how to cook—the way they learned from their parents and grandparents, and so on, generation after generation in China.

Unfortunately, I didn't learn to cook very well. In fact, one day a friend of mine actually spit out a cookie that I had baked.

When I cook for my own family nowadays, I usually start with a recipe found in a book or online. But then, even though I know I should follow the directions, something takes over and I can't help but improvise: a pinch more spice, a hotter oven, a shorter cooking time, a few extra spoonfuls of oil. The way I feel compelled to deviate from the recipe, it's almost as if I am a marionette—and, in heaven, GongGong and PoPo are looking down, shaking their heads, wishing they could pull the strings.

How does your family like to cook?
With precision or inspiration or a little of both?
How about you?

Marathon

I hope the Chinese
wins the race.

I see myself
in her face.

Does she see me
in this crowd?

Does she hear me
cheering loud?

When I am grown
but not too old—

I'll run this race.
And win the gold.

When I was young, whenever the Olympics or another international sports competition was on TV, my father would keep an eye out for the Chinese athletes and point in excitement. If the Chinese athlete won, he would shout, "Look! Look! Did you see? She's CHINESE!" I usually would just roll my eyes—because I always felt more American than Chinese.

But if an athlete were Asian American, then that was a different story. Even if the athlete looked completely different from me—as they usually did, since I have never been athletic—I would still feel like I was looking in a mirror. Or looking at a cousin, or a best friend.

That being said, I think my favorite Olympian is Usain Bolt, who is not remotely like me at all. I admire his speed and power. More than that, I love the relaxed way he looks around mid-stride, where his joy for running really comes through. Go, Jamaica!

During the Olympics or other world competitions, who do you cheer for?

Part 3:
AMERICAN POEMS

Half and Half

I AM AMERICAN. I was born here, in Los Angeles, in the old Queen of Angels Hospital, right off the 101 freeway. Four years ago they boarded up the building. I read it might be rented out as a movie studio next year.

Sometimes the first question a stranger will ask me, even before learning my name, is "What are you?" or "Where are you from?" These kinds of people usually stare hard at my face, as if they are testing themselves on how well they can tell the difference between Chinese and Korean and Japanese. Usually I give them what they want to know, quickly, and get it over with. It can be fun, though, to pretend I do not understand.

My mother says when I was six years old I got in a big fight with our neighbors. Carol and Daryl had teased me for being half Chinese and half Korean. They were full-blooded Japanese Americans and called me a half-breed, a mixed poodle. We *did* have a mixed poodle then, Blackie. My mother says I cried, and she laughs, patting my curly permed hair.

Some non-Asian people look at Asians and lump us all together. Japanese, Chinese, Korean: they think we are the same. There are some similarities among these cultures, but there are also enormous differences—and a history of war between Japan, China, and Korea. Even today, a Japanese person is likely to encounter some bias in China, and a Korean person might feel discriminated against in Japan.

When I was a child living on Catalina Street in Los Angeles, Carol and Daryl, so proud of being Japanese, were really mean about teasing me for being half Chinese and half Korean. The odd thing is that most of my father's friends at the time were Japanese American. His best friend Shin worked at their family factory, Umeya Rice Cake Co. in Little Tokyo, and we would visit often to buy snacks there and paper goods at Bunkado next door. I even took karate in Little Tokyo. In a way, I was almost part Japanese, too.

Carol and Daryl: if you are reading this now, it is all right to feel bad—really, really bad. You also used to make fun of me for not being able to climb the laundry pole and the big tree behind our apartment building. Do you remember? I do.

Does your ethnicity match up
with the culture(s) that you are most interested in?

MANNERS

If you are Chinese
and you eat out of
a porcelain bowl,
you may pick it up
and push the rice
into your mouth
with your chopsticks,
feeling a bit like
a pig, digging in.
But it is okay,
if you are Chinese.

If you are Korean,
though, you must
leave your stainless
steel bowl sitting
on the table, even
if it has gone cold
while you barbecue
beef for your father.

And if you are half
and half, like me,
born in L.A. and hungry
all the time,
you might wonder
if you aren't better off
sticking with
a knife and fork.

If you opened the kitchen cabinets in my house when I was growing up, you would find a mishmash of dishes: colorful Chinese plastic dishes, delicate blue-and-white Japanese porcelain bowls and plates, a few Korean metal rice bowls, lots of sturdy CorningWare, and souvenir coffee cups from Solvang.

The dishes matched our diet. We ate all kinds of food, not just Chinese and Korean, but burgers, spaghetti, pizza, tacos, sushi, tempura, Danish butter cookies. My mother's favorite food for a while was Salvadoran pupusas, which we bought from a food truck downtown. My favorite foods were shrimp dumplings, wonton noodle soup, shrimp tempura, french fries, my mother's potato salad, hash browns, and potato chips.

I often carry a potato in the Poetry Suitcase that I bring to schools, and even just looking at it makes me happy. I think I need to put a plastic shrimp in there, too.

If we opened your kitchen cabinets at home,
what would it tell us about your family?
What are your favorite foods?

Face It

My nose belongs
to Guangdong, China—
short and round, a Jang family nose.

My eyes belong
to Alsace, France—
wide like Grandmother Hemmerling's.

But my mouth, my big-talking mouth, belongs
to me, alone.

This poem is about my son. One week after he was born, I brought him to my Chinese grandfather's house. GongGong lived at that time in the Los Feliz area of Los Angeles, near Griffith Park, just a few miles from where I was living (in Silver Lake). GongGong took one look at Andrew and exclaimed, "One hundred percent Chinese!"

I corrected him. "Well, no, GongGong—Andrew is one quarter Chinese, one quarter Korean, one quarter French, and one quarter German. Look at his big eyes! He gets those from Glenn's side."

GongGong dismissed the thought. "We have BIG eyes, too!" he shouted with pride, opening his eyes so wide and round that they looked as if they were going to pop out of his face.

Every once in a while my husband and I like to joke that Andrew's various personality traits come from different relatives—his ability to chat with strangers comes from Grandpa, and his love of clever gadgets comes from Grandy. Mainly, though, I still find myself marveling at the way he has become his own unique self; his mouth really does belong to him alone.

How are you similar to your family members,
either in appearance or personality?
In what ways are you one hundred percent original?

OTHER

We notice each other right away.
We are the only two Asians in the room.
It does not matter that her hair is long.
It does not matter that I am fat.
I look at her like I look in a mirror,
recognizing my self in one quick glance.

While I might notice the only other Asian in a room right away, I might not bond with him or her. If she is a very fancy person, with high heels and makeup—one of the pampered women in *Crazy Rich Asians*—we'll notice each other but probably won't like each other, because I am a very casual person and rather plain in my lifestyle. If she doesn't like eating, we almost definitely won't bond, because I am constantly thinking about food, talking about food, or eating. A friend once told me, "You are the only person I know who thinks about dinner while you're eating breakfast." My true identity? I am an Eater.

When I visited a school in Beijing, I stayed at a hotel where almost everyone was Asian. At the buffet breakfast in the hotel dining room, there was a line. I stood in line along with several Asian businessmen. When it was my turn to be seated, the Chinese hostess looked through me and signaled to a man behind me to follow her. I was so angry. She might've skipped me for any number of reasons, but I felt that it was because I was a woman.

I argued—peacefully, but loudly enough so that a white woman seated near us happened to hear. From her casual clothes and the food piled high on her plate, I guessed that she was American (and a person, like me, who liked eating). She and I made eye contact. I felt comforted to have another Other who understood.

What is your true identity?
When you walk into a room,
who do you notice right away?

Which?

Two dresses hang
side by side
on the sale rack,
the tag of one so worn
it seems the price
was not believed,
but looked at, at least twice,
by many who might buy.

It is real: this
black velvet gown
overgrown with
lush, bright flowers
is cheap, dirt cheap,
even cheaper than
the simple chambray dress
some careless hand
has pressed up against its back,
the white plastic hanger
crushing one velvet flower.

Which one is you?
Wear this plain blue frock
twice a week and feel safe,
no one will talk;
but wear the other,
with its strange power
that makes you think
the boys will swoon,

and a second time
a season
is too soon.

Summer between sixth and seventh grade, I lived with my Chinese grandparents. PoPo and I often went shopping for clothes. Most days we would just look, see what was out there, try things on, and think about what we might want to buy later, especially if it went on sale.

After weeks of comparison shopping, I decided that I really wanted to buy a shiny black velvet jacket at Sears. It had elbow-length sleeves with snazzy upturned cuffs and a stylish wide lapel, but what made it so special were the huge, brightly colored flowers printed on it. They really popped against the black velvet. It was the most expensive piece of clothing that I would own up until that point. If I remember, it was about thirty dollars. PoPo bought it for me, along with a few other pieces like a plain navy blue cotton twill jacket with metal buttons that said "Winnie the Pooh." I didn't really want the blue jacket, but PoPo said it was practical.

When my parents came to pick me up the weekend before the start of school, I put on a little "fashion show" for them. My father looked at my velvet jacket, pointed, and yelled, "Oh, boy, THAT is LOUD!" Everyone in the room laughed (except for me and PoPo). The laughter seemed to go on for a long time, slo-mo laughter, my uncles and my mother and everyone pointing at me in my jacket. I felt so stupid. I never put the jacket on again, but kept it in the back of my closet until I graduated from high school, when I gave it to Goodwill. I hope that someone found it for a dollar, and loved it, and wore it many times.

Do you have a favorite piece of clothing?
What does it say about you?

QUITTER

Coach calls me a quitter.

He mutters it under his breath
loud enough for me to hear,
but quiet enough
so no one knows
when I prove him wrong.

Junior year of high school, we had a tough gym teacher. He made us run on the hottest days till we dropped—or vomited, or cried, or bled. I often had nose bleeds, bad ones. Nothing would make the blood stop for ten or fifteen minutes. I'd plug my nostrils with tissue and tip my head back, pressing hard at the bridge of my nose and swallowing clots of blood. This was when I lived in Walnut, where Stage 1 Smog Alerts are common. We'd be struggling, wheezing in the thick, brown, soupy air, but our P.E. teacher didn't care. Worse yet, maybe, he did care; I think he wanted us to struggle because he thought it would make us stronger.

In a weird way, it did make me stronger. I decided to start running at night, when it was easier to breathe, so I could build up my stamina and then run during P.E. without embarrassing myself. I started with a mile, then two, and worked my way up to five miles a night. Then I made my mistake. I told my parents I wanted to try out for the cross country team.

I'll remind you: I was a little plump. My mother would say "chubby" or "roly-poly"; my father just used the word "fat," very often in the phrase, "Move your fat ***" (even though it was my belly that was fat, not my rear). I had lost weight from the nightly running, but they didn't notice. In fact, they seemed to have forgotten that I had been doing nightly running at all when they said, *Track team? You gotta be kidding. You're so slow. You can't run.* So I quit thinking about it. Just like that, I quit before I even got started.

Is there something you would like to try to do?
Where can you find support
to help you make it happen?

OUR DAILY BREAD

Nine P.M. we close the store,
wash the counter, mop the floor.

Ten P.M. we finally eat.
Father pulls a milk crate seat

to the table and we pray.
Thank you for this crazy day.

My family owned a series of small businesses when I was growing up. None of the businesses was profitable. Yes, they all made money, but we worked so many hours a week—everyone chipping in, hardly any free time—it seemed we were working like mad just to earn the minimum wage.

In high school I wanted desperately to get a "normal" summer job at McDonald's. Instead, my parents had me working at our sewing factory. One day I was the bundle girl (bundling parts of clothes), the next day I was the trimming girl (trimming loose threads) or the plancha girl (ironing the clothes)—helping out where needed.

The last business that my parents owned was Tri-City Market in Myrtle Creek, Oregon. I was already an adult when they bought it, but I wasn't able to avoid working there. When I took my son to visit Grandma and Grandpa, the three of them would fish in the local river or go crabbing at Coos Bay—and I would stay and run the store. Work started at 6 A.M., making coffee and filling the soda machine with ice. My parents would usually stick around to cook Chinese food for the "to-go" steam table before lunch, but I'd need to stir fry a wok full of replacement food if someone bought it all. (Pity the people who ate my food.)

It was not uncommon for us to sit and eat dinner at 10 P.M., or even later. We'd use milk crates stacked double-high for seats and scarf down the food, one eye on the register and an ear out for the bell on the door. Those days were not just crazy, they were *insane*.

What is work like for your family?
What is the hardest work you've ever had to do?
What would you rather have done instead?

TREAT

It's my best friend's treat.
I won our bet.

I'd love the shrimp,
but I think I'll get
the pork instead—
it's half the price.

It's my best friend's treat,
but I'll treat her nice.

I love shrimp. If I were a flamingo, I would be very pink. But I might not order shrimp if a friend is paying. I always feel that I should rein myself in a bit when friends pay, and order something cheap. I like picking up the bill for everyone when I go out. It makes me feel free to eat whatever I want.

I used to have a hard time eating at an expensive restaurant. I might enjoy the food, but then I would start to think, "I could've bought a pair of shoes for the cost of this meal!" or "I could've bought five books!" Anyway, the most expensive meal isn't always the best. One of my favorite meals is a "picnic dinner" of salami, cheese, bread, and fruit. And pour me a glass of homemade lemonade!

What are some of your favorite expensive foods?
How about your favorite inexpensive foods?

LOTTO

My brother buys tickets
every Wednesday.
He scrounges change,
rummaging through
coat pockets
and old purses
in the closet,
turning over
couch cushions,
checking the
coin return slots
of copy machines
and pay phones.
We pass a penny,
he picks it up.
And all week long
we wait for luck.

If I were to search my house for spare change right now, I might find about twenty dollars here and there. A fortune compared to what I used to find when I was a kid. Back then, I searched my house for money every few weeks, but mainly just found coins that had fallen out of my father's pockets into the spaces between the couch cushions. I'd get better results at the supermarket—I could usually find something in the coin return slots of copy machines or pay phones.

My mother says that when I was four years old, I used to talk about buying a big new house for her. If I had won a thousand dollars as a kid, I would've kept a hundred and given the rest to my mom because it made me sad when she talked about being poor.

Shortly after she came to visit us in California, we took my Korean grandmother to Disneyland. We bought pizza for lunch. "PIZ-ZA," I said slowly, pointing to it. It was the first time she had ever seen it. She nodded vigorously and said, "PI-JA!" Halmoni had said the Korean word for "expensive." My mother laughed harder than I'd ever seen her laugh.

And, yes, Disneyland pizza is some of the most expensive pizza I've ever had.

Is money important to your family?
Do they talk about it all the time?
What is most important to you?

IN THE NEIGHBORHOOD

We drove past
our old house
today.
The redwood
fence is warped
and gray.
The tree
I planted
grew so tall
it makes
our house look
plain and small.

When we
lived there,
it was the best.
Now it seems
just like
the rest.

We moved a lot when I was kid. I lived in seven different places—five apartments, two houses—by the time I graduated from high school. My favorite home by far was our Oak Springs Drive house in San Anselmo, California. We had a yard! I loved it.

If you were to enter the address of that house online, you would see a photo of the back of it, just a little bit of the roof showing above a redwood fence. When my son was in high school, we were in the area for a tournament, so I took him there. I wanted him to see my favorite childhood home. I knocked on the door to ask if we could look at the back yard, to see the fruit trees that we had planted. The man who answered the door looked at us as if we were criminals. I explained that this had been my house when I was in third through sixth grades—and my father and I had built the redwood fence in back. He snapped, "No, you didn't!" I said, "Pardon me?" He shouted, "Don't lie! I built that fence." I didn't know what to say. Quietly, I asked, "Was the old redwood fence falling down? Did you replace it?" He glared at me and threatened to call the police.

Catching a glimpse of old Mr. Campbell-Walker across the street, I scurried over to re-introduce myself. He remembered me as the girl in the Asian family that lived there a long time ago. I asked if he remembered throwing me into his swimming pool when I was eight. (I almost drowned.) He wasn't sure that he remembered that part. My son shook his head, pretending not to know me.

What memories do you have
of the places where you've lived?
What do you remember about your favorite home?

STRAIGHT A'S

My parents and I
don't talk about grades.
It's understood.
I will get A's.

They never say what
they want me to do.
I wish they would—
I wish I knew.

I received very little praise—or even pressure—from my parents on the subject of grades. Thinking back, I'm not sure how I knew that I needed to bring home A's. I just guessed— or felt, deep inside—that it was important to do well, to make them proud. Children of poor immigrant parents often feel this way. We see our parents working so hard. They look so tired. Everything that they are doing is for us. They talk about their sacrifices and we can't help but feel guilty. I put the pressure to get good grades on myself.

Many recent Asian immigrants to this country weren't poor and uneducated in their home countries. They came to America for graduate school. They work in professional jobs. I imagine that there is a different feeling of pressure to get good grades if you are a child whose parents went to a top university. It might not be easy, feeling that you need to live up to your family's standards.

Some schools are going "gradeless" or almost gradeless, asking students to do self-evaluations. I'm not sure that a self-evaluation system would've worked for me. If I did poorly in a class, could I really give myself a C?

Do you think a gradeless school would work?
Or do you think that the pressure of grades helps you learn?

BEAT

When I was small
they spanked me
with a newspaper
rolled tight,
and I would yell
until the neighbors
opened their warped
wooden windows.

Now they have learned
a better way,
and the pain hurts worse
than a whipping
when they shake
their heads, whispering,
"We are so ashamed,"
in a room so quiet
you hear them
swallow.

My mother was beaten often as a child. She never went into it in detail, but told me enough that I figured it out myself.

My father was chased out of his home by my grandfather, who threatened him with a butcher knife. What terrible thing had he done wrong to merit being thrown out of the house? He had just gone to the movies with his friends, without permission.

My grandfather's strongest memory of school was of his teacher hitting him repeatedly on his hands with a stick. For "being stupid." He retaliated by farting on his teacher's rice when no one was looking.

I got spanked with a newspaper from time to time, but that was an easy punishment. It didn't really hurt that much. What hurt most was knowing that I had done something to disappoint my parents. The newspaper wasn't even necessary.

The worst thing that I did to my son when he was a kid was to yell at him and call him a "dead fish" (for having no energy at a tournament). Once in a while, he still brings that up. I think he'll still be reminding me of that when I'm eighty years old.

Think about a time when you have made a mistake
or have wrongly been accused of doing something bad.
Could anything have changed the way you acted?

QUILT

Our family
is a quilt

of odd remnants
patched together

in a strange
pattern,

threads fraying,
fabric wearing thin—

but made to keep
its warmth

even in bitter
cold.

PoPo:
The blue twill of my Winnie-the-Pooh jacket.

GongGong:
The canvas he learned to paint on when he was 88.

My Korean grandparents, Halmoni and Haraboji:
Stiff beige linen, the clothes of old-time farmers.

My father:
Wide-wale corduroy.
A life of ups and downs.

My mother:
An ivory-colored vinyl tablecloth, embossed with flowers.
A cigarette burn in it.

Me:
Boiled wool.

All of us, now and then:
Rough patches.

Swatches of smooth silk:
we can hope.

What kind of fabrics
might you choose for your family?
For you?

ADVICE
FOR WRITERS

Just Try

I wrote *A Suitcase of Seaweed* between the hours of 9 P.M. and 2 A.M. in 1993 and 1994, from when my son was two months old until he turned one year old. He was not a napper, so I was always exhausted when I sat down at my computer. Crummy stuff stuttered out of my fingers for the first hour. The quality of my writing started getting better around midnight. By 2 A.M. I was convinced that I was a genius. I would've kept writing until dawn, except I needed at least a few hours of rest to get me through the next day.

I often meet people who say, "I'd love to be a writer, but I don't have the time." Start small. Wake up one hour early on Saturday and Sunday. Something will flow out of your fingers. Don't judge it yet. You don't need complete sentences. Take quick notes of whatever you find in your mind at the moment. *Ice cream - plop - sidewalk. Ants - legs - screaming.*

Five minutes at a time—when you get to school early, when dinner's not ready, when you're waiting for your favorite TV show, when you can't fall asleep at night—revisit your work. Don't try to make it better, just make it different. Even when you love a first draft, write four or five drafts to give yourself a choice. Take the best parts of each draft and stitch them together. I believe we're never truly "done" with a piece of writing. It's not like a race with a finish line or a turkey with a pop-up button. It's all about revising (and revising) until we need to stop. Five minutes at a time, you can write something good.

If you wanted to be a high school basketball star, you wouldn't limit yourself to playing games at school. You'd build your skills, dribbling the ball until it drove your neighbors crazy, shooting hoops past dark. Writing is the same way. If you want to be the best writer that you can be, you need to put in your own time to build your skills. It doesn't need to be a lot of time. In five minutes, you can write a draft of a poem. If you want to be a screenwriter, or a car reviewer, or a cancer researcher who needs to write million dollar grant proposals, poetry can help you. Writing poetry is like doing sit-ups for the mind.

TRADITIONAL PUBLISHING

If you want to get published the traditional way, you'll find dozens of books to teach you the steps. Go to your school library and also your public library; you'll find different things in each place. Get to know your librarians. Tell them that you're interested in becoming a writer. Ask for help.

They will point you to shelves of books on everything from writing screenplays for movies, to writing sports articles for magazines, to writing lyrics for songs, to writing books for children and teens. If you love playing video games, look for books on video game storytelling. There is a book out there for almost any kind of writing that you might want to do. If it's not at one of your libraries, look on Amazon; if you find something that looks useful, see if the public library can get it for you somehow, perhaps through interlibrary loan.

If writing a book is your goal, then when you're ready, you can start sending your writing to publishers. How do you choose a publisher? The how-to books have lots of tips, but I think a good way to find a compatible publisher is to look at your favorite new books and see who published them. Look at publishers' tweets to see what they're excited about. Read interviews with authors and editors. If one of your favorite publishing houses is accepting unsolicited submissions, BINGO! Send your manuscript in. If they are only accepting agented submissions, you can try to get an agent —there are books on that—or you can do more research to find publishers that are open to considering manuscripts from writers that they don't know.

Then wait. Be prepared to wait for months, even more than a year sometimes. While you're waiting, start writing something new. Your second book. Your third book. Dr. Seuss received many, many rejections before his first book was sold. Even J.K. Rowling received rejection letters. Can you imagine how you would feel today if you were one of the editors who said no to Harry Potter? You might just be the next Dr. Seuss. The next J.K. Rowling. Or the very first YOU!

Indie Publishing

If a few years pass and you haven't been able to get your writing published the traditional way, you might want to think about indie publishing, also called self-publishing or POD (print-on-demand) publishing. My first twenty-one books were all published traditionally by publishers such as Harcourt and FSG. I got into indie publishing when, after the retirement of my editor Margaret McElderry, *A Suitcase of Seaweed* was put out of print. People said, "Tell Simon & Schuster that we love this book!" Unfortunately, it doesn't work that way. Think of all the books that you loved as a child; chances are, at least half of them are out of print now. Some books go out of print after just a year or two. *A Suitcase of Seaweed* was in print for more than ten years.

When my first several books went out of print, I created paperback versions that were sold by CreateSpace, a company owned by Amazon. Recently Amazon moved most of their print-on-demand operations to Kindle Direct Publishing (KDP), which has handled their ebook publishing for a while. Here's a summary of the KDP process. Read more, if you're interested, at various blogs online.

1) create a free account at KDP;

2) enter info for the book you're creating (title, author, subject, trim size, black-and-white or color, price, etc.);

3) upload a PDF of the interior of the book;

4) upload a PDF of the cover; and

5) submit your book for review.

When your book passes review, it will go up at Amazon.com. You can send the link to everyone you know—and see who your true friends are! If your book becomes a bestseller, it's possible that you will receive an offer from a traditional publisher for the same book (or your next book). You might even land a movie deal! All you need to do is . . . get writing.

Next Saturday morning, get up an hour early. I'll be thinking of you.

Janet Wong is a graduate of Yale Law School and a former lawyer who switched careers to become a children's author. Her dramatic career change has been featured on *The Oprah Winfrey Show*, CNN's *Paula Zahn Show*, and *Radical Sabbatical*. She is the author of more than 30 books for children and teens on a wide variety of subjects, including writing and revision (*You Have to Write*), diversity and community (*Apple Pie 4th of July*), peer pressure (*Me and Rolly Maloo*), chess (*Alex and the Wednesday Chess Club*), and yoga (*Twist: Yoga Poems*). A frequent featured speaker at literacy conferences, Wong has served as a member of several national committees, including the NCTE Poetry Committee and the ILA Notable Books for a Global Society committee.

Her two main interests now are publishing anthologies (with her colleague Sylvia Vardell) to make it easy for teachers to share poetry with students, and encouraging children and teens to publish their own writing using affordable new technologies.

You can find more info about Janet Wong at **JanetWong.com**. Read about her work with Sylvia Vardell at **PomeloBooks.com**.

BOOKS BY VARDELL & WONG

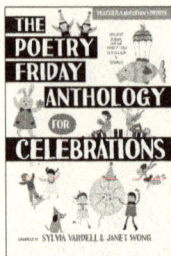

The Poetry Friday Anthology for Celebrations
ILA 2016 Notable Books for a Global Society

Teacher/Librarian Edition (K-8)
Each of the 156 poems has a *Take 5!* mini-lesson with picture book pairings.
Matrixes highlight social studies and language arts connections.

Student Edition (K-8)
This companion volume for children features illustrations (no mini-lessons).
Listen to 35 poems in Spanish & English—FREE at SoundCloud.com!

"A bubbly and educational bilingual poetry anthology for children." —*Kirkus*

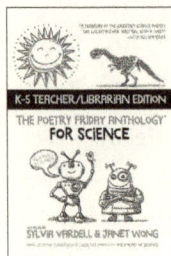

The Poetry Friday Anthology for Science
NSTA Recommends
Featured on ScienceFriday.com + in a monthly column in *Science & Children*
250+ poems on science, technology, engineering, and math

K-5 Teacher/Librarian Edition (K-5)
Each poem is accompanied by a *Take 5!* mini-lesson with both language arts
and science-themed teaching tips.

Student Edition (K-8)
The Poetry of Science is an illustrated companion volume for children that is
organized by topic and features illustrations (no mini-lessons).

**"A treasury of the greatest science poetry for children ever written,
with a twist" —NSTA Recommends**

Common Core TEKS

The Poetry Friday Anthology (K-5 Teacher Edition)

A Children's Poet Laureate Pick of the List
36 poems per grade level (K-5) on a wide variety of themes, with
Take 5! mini-lessons that highlight poetry skills and standards.

The Poetry Friday Anthology for Middle School
(Grades 6-8 Teacher Edition)

An NCTE Poetry Notable
36 poems per grade level (grades 6-8) on a wide variety of themes,
with *Take 5!* mini-lessons that highlight poetry skills and standards.

Available in a Common Core version or a TEKS version

You Just Wait: A Poetry Friday Power Book
(Grades 5 and up)
An NCTE Poetry Notable

This interactive story in poems and writing journal centers around identity, diversity, movies, and sports (soccer and basketball). Extensive back matter resources for readers and writers.

> **"This delightful collection . . . makes both reading and writing poetry personal and accessible to even the most resistant."**
> —*School Library Journal*

Here We Go: A Poetry Friday Power Book
(Grades 3 and up)
An NCTE Poetry Notable
An NNSTOY Social Justice Book

This interactive story inspires kids with themes of diversity and social activism (organizing a walkathon, canned food drive, and school garden). Extensive back matter resources for young writers and kids who want to change the world.

> **"Filled with poems by a variety of award-winning poets, this engaging resource invites readers to 'power up' and explore the world of poetry."**—*Literacy Daily*

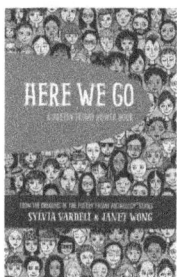

Pet Crazy: A Poetry Friday Power Book
(Grades K-4)
A CBC Hot Off the Press selection

This interactive story—with Hidden Language Skills that engage kids in "playing" with punctuation, spelling, and other basics—features three characters who love spending time with animals. Extensive back matter features resources for helping young people perform, read, write, and try to publish poetry.

> **"An enthusiastic invitation for kids to celebrate their animal friends through poetry composition."**—*Kirkus*

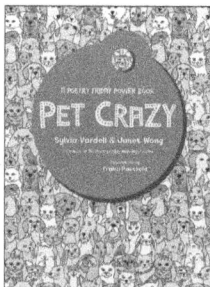

FIND SAMPLE POEMS AT PINTEREST.COM/POMELOBOOKS
& AT POMELOBOOKS.COM